JOURNEYS THROUGH UNSEEN SOULS

FRANK D. ROBINSON

ISBN:0615726372

ISBN-13: 978-0615726373

TABLE OF CONTENT

Note to the reader

Falling in love inhabits a special place. It brings together human companionship to fuel the heart and everyday this is tested by wealth, fame, poverty and ethics. Therefore, love moves in the direction of universal transition between two people surpassing all material things to bring about a union which can survive in prosperity.

-I miss you-

I miss you everyday
My heart and soul
Feels wrapped up
In a cocoon of pain
If I could pull you
From my memories
I would do it again
To feel your love
From the time it began
Your touch, your eyes
Embedded in my mind
I love you too much
To leave it all behind

Do you remember?-

Do you remember the day?
Words were found to say

The sun grew bright to see
Time was there for us to meet

Do you remember the night?
Our first kiss under the light

The moon was bright to see
Our hearts had time to meet

Do you remember the way?
We found this love to stay

Having the past to retrieve
Adds another day we can see

-Mama you should know-

Mama the news is grim
As my life slowly dims
The pain leaves me weak
Making it hard to speak
You showed me love
More than enough
When in heaven
I'll still know how much
Mama don't cry no more
Because I'm sick and sore
You gave me life
The courage to fight
My eyes will soon close
For eternity I will know
You're the greatest mother
A son could ever know

-My only wish-

If I had one wish
One wish come true
To see my days
Growing old with you

To have one chance
One chance comes true
Devoting my heart
Forever loving you

-Timeless love-

You're my timeless love
You're my best friend
To journey through life
From beginning to end
Since the day we met
My dreams came true
Every part of my soul
Fell in love with you
You're my timeless love
You're my best friend
The heart in my chest
From beginning to end

Frank D. Robinson

-A tiny life begins-

Your birth begins a life today
Growing step by step each day

Another family name to see
Making you part of the family tree

You came from love
A bundle of joy we received

Your time will come to move away
Taking our love to stay

The future is yours to make
Until such time, you are here today

We love you with all our heart
We will never be far apart

-Words from a little angel-

I've seen pictures of a special land
Daddy you call it heaven
Soon our lord will guide my hand
I know you think this is mean
But mommy is there waiting for me
You guided my life from the start
When I was born with a beating heart
Where I'm going there is no goodbye
Daddy you call it heaven
Mommy and I will meet you in the sky

-Sacrifice-

To sacrifice my only soul
To bring about two as whole
To sacrifice my only heart
To share love in equal parts
I'll give my all to sacrifice
If you'll be my loving wife

Note to the reader

Love has a unique and special way of showing itself for someone you truly love. It brings back times of fun, laughter, joy and passion for one another. The distance between two hearts does not matter; one may be further than the other but memories of being together live within the heart.

-Last days-

The sickness breaks me down
From within and around
My strength is almost gone
Pain from dusk till dawn
Life is slowly escaping me
Soon my spirit shall be free
Every day I know it's more
My body weak and sore
Tears and fears each day
Soon will be my yesterday
Hand in hand I will stand
With family and friends
Among his promise land

-So deeply-

I love you so deeply,
And way too much
The warmth in your eyes
And the way we touch
How you make me smile
In your own special way,
The joy that you bring
Into our lives everyday
I love who you are
As it was from the start,
Together now and forever
With all my heart

-Seasons change with passing days-

Seasons change with passing days
The same for love in different ways

Warm as summer, we can believe
Or cold as winter some receive

Seasons change with passing days
Feelings follow in many ways

Colorful as fall may bring
Or unstable as spring can be

Seasons change with passing days
So do lives in different ways

The future lies beyond our sight
Leaving us to unknown life

-Glowing soul-

Your beauty is evermore
Upon loves peaceful shore
Glowing with a soul
Unlike any I seen before
Within my heart
Love grew from the start
You're all that I need
And everything in between
The true meaning of evermore
Upon loves peaceful shore

-Mind of memories-

In my mind of memories
You can never be erased
So special and valuable
No person can replace
Although in my eyes
I seen you as dad
You were always there
If I was happy or sad
The world's greatest father
This child could ever know
Part of me left with you
So in heaven you're not alone

-Wedding day-

On this our wedding day
We start our second life
Two souls become entwined
One groom, one bride
Life comes with challenges
It often does for all
Love will be our strength
To never let each other fall
Sharing joy and memories
As they come our way
Keeping them forever close
In our hearts each day

-You are the one-

You are the one
Who stole my heart?
To be my everything
You are the one
Who became my reality?
You bring beauty to life
In mind, in soul, and body
You are the one
My dreams, my fantasy
From the beginning
You touched my soul
With nothing but love
You flew down from above
For me to love and hold

-The forgotten-

Do you feel the pain I hide?
Moving and burning inside
It's pure, it's alive
Do you see it in my eyes?
Do you care if a child cries?
Behind windows and walls
Of false perceptions
Building in my skull
Do you know who I am?
This reality that exists
An orphan child
Who never asked for this!

-In loving memory-

We thought of you with love today
In our hearts we do
The same as yesterday
And every day before that too
In silence or mourning
Family and friends say your name
Together with everlasting memories
Your picture in a frame
Your love is our keepsake
With which we will never part
God holds you in his safekeeping
Thou you are in our hearts

Note to the reader

Babies are little angels with no wings. Something special unfolds when parents interact with a baby it opens a magical spot in us. As they stare at us with curious little eyes and a tiny little smile, we look back into their eyes and see how special and meaningful life really is. It all begins with little angels with no wings.

-She found her hero-

She found her hero
Far from zero
A father who cares
And is always there
When she is sad
He is dad
When there is a frown
He turns it around
Someone who stayed
And never walked away
She grew to shine
With the passing of time
Now a woman
In her father's eyes

The greatest gift-

A baby is the greatest gift
Heaven can bestow
A special time in life
Two parents will forever know
Sharing each moment of happiness
That love can only touch
With the help of family
To understand how much
A beautiful creation
Worth more than gold
The greatest treasure
Two parents can hold

-Falling rain-

When the rain falls
Visions of you come into view
It reminds me of teardrops
That I cried for two
I miss you even more
When there is no rain
I'll never forget your love
That took my breath away
My days are left in sadness
Since you passed away
Heaven separated us in life
Until I'm yours again someday

-Cupid's arrow-

When it comes to cupid's arrow
It hit us in the rear
Evoking love and happiness
Between us to share
We found a special relationship
It's ours to understand
Entwining two souls
Side by side, hand in hand
Together in this world
There is no I in team
It takes the power of love
To make a perfect "we"

-Daddy's little girl-

In the arms of an angel
Heaven took you from me
Daddy's little girl
In ribbons and curls
Looking up to the sky
It's hard not to cry
When I sing you this song
Titled "My little butterfly"
Forgive me if I weep
Because it hurts very deep
You were my world
Daddy's little girl

TABLE OF CONTENTS

-My Juliet-

I have read many things
Like Romeo and Juliet
Small romantic parts
Romeo said when they met
Her beauty he seen
Both near and far
She became his queen
And the key to his heart
I feel the same way
To call you my Juliet
Who lives inside me?
Since the day we met

-The sweetest man-

He holds me when I cry
Turns my frowns upside down
One hope, one dream
My strength to believe
He wipes away my tears
And kisses away the fears
One heart, one soul
My eternal love to hold
I love him without regret
The sweetest man I ever met

-Missing you-

I know you're in a loving place
Part of me went too
Knowing you're happy there
I still cry from missing you
My soul feels so empty
As I try to carry on
You were my heart
But now you are gone
I will always think of you
Until we meet high above
There we can have eternity
Embracing each other's love

-Our angel-

Today as you lay asleep
In your hospital bed
There is a mix of love
And rejoice to be said
From your cute little face
And beautiful tiny eyes
No words can truly define
Our heartfelt emotions inside
The wait is finally over
Our angel arrived today
Filling our hearts with joy
And memories to last and stay

-Can I be your teddy bear?-

Can I be your teddy bear?
Stuff my chest with care
Stitch me up over time
Every touch makes me
Feel more and more alive
Give me eyes you truly desire
To see your beauty to admire
Remember to give me a heart
To love you from the start
Can I be your teddy bear?
Soft and gentle, always near
To know your special touch
And to feel your love so much

-You are not alone-

You are not alone
I'm there with you
In a night or in a day
Near your side
I never flew away
Every gentle breeze
Or raindrop you see
They come from above
My touch, my tears
To the woman I love

-Peace in my soul-

There is peace in my soul
Opening like a blooming rose
So much love in my life
A love of harmony and
Security you show
You took hold of my heart
More than any could reach
I finally knew then
Love found its way to me
You gave me a new life
I never felt more complete
From that day on
You became my inner peace

-A promise-

I give you all of me
As a devotion to you
A promise I'll be here
This journey for two
My arms to hold you
If life seems dark and gray
And I will comfort you
While the night melts away
I promise here and now
One thing is true
My heart and soul
Is here to always love you

-Be not afraid-

An angel whispered
Your time here is done
Be not afraid of death
Your life only just begun
You will know a special place
Free from pain and tears
Replaced by laughter and smiles
From family who are there
To welcome you home above
With everlasting happiness
And eternal love

-Something about him-

A soft brush of his fingertips
Moving up and down my spine
Came with love amid his eyes
There was love equaling mine
He always makes me happy
And warms my heart with a kiss
If we were apart too long
My soul would feel amiss
Maybe it's his eyes
Or they way he cares for me
But whatever it is
I love him beyond belief

-I Surrender-

Your love is like an ocean
Laying in my chest so deep
You're like a purple rose
Whose beauty is complete?
Your love is like the stars
That never seems to end
You're like an angel
With a loving soul to send
To you my heart belongs
A journey to take together
Our time is here and now
It's to you that I surrender

-Your angel wings-

Here's a set of angel wings
And your white halo too
You deserve each one
For all the things you do
You bring happiness to my days
And show your loving care
When I need you by my side
You find a way to be there
A set of wings are special
And a white halo is too
I found me an angel
There is none like you

-Dear mom-

Dear mom, I said a prayer for you
To thank our lord above
For giving us another year
Of never ending love
I'm thankful for the caring
You've shown from year to year
And the bond we have
In times of happiness and tears
Thank you from the heart
For always being there
I'm forever grateful
For a mother who truly cares

-I Gave-

I gave you my heart
So I may love you
From the very start
I gave you my soul
Something special
Only you can hold
Standing before you
I found a new life
We created together
But now I must ask
Will you be my wife?

-Fate-

Was it fate that we met?
Standing beneath the rain
The two of us dripping wet
Someone from my dreams
Now a reality
But as time passed by
Love became much more
You moved my soul
Unlike anything I felt before
I never believed in fate
Until it came from a dream
From heaven high above
An angel was sent to me

-Determine the words-

Determine the words poets speak
To open their world for you to see

Words are used from life they seen
Some are true, others false to read

Determine the words poets will say
Leaving us to read their lives today

Some write books, leaving us fantasy
Others have left their hopes and dreams

Determine the words poets speak
Some are personal for us to read

Their minds will travel from day to day
Speaking out in words to see today

-In my life-

You came into my life
There was no mistake
The only one
Keeping my heart awake
It's because of you
When I frown
Your beauty and love
Turns it upside down
You came into my life
There was no mistake
The only one
Keeping my soul awake

-Greatest artist-

God is the greatest artist
No other name compares
He gave us beautiful sunsets
To gaze upon and share
Creating lands and oceans
And splendid skies above
Adding trees and flowers
A work of art we can love
All around the world
Everything was done with care
He made us a beautiful world
To gaze upon and share

-Earth and heaven-

Our hearts feel broken
Heavy in deep despair
To lose someone we love
It comes with tears
They're gone from this earth
Beyond human sight
To live in our lord's kingdom
Sharing his eternal light
A journey we make
To be in heaven above
Where family awaits
With open arms and love

-You changed my world-

You changed my world
In a blink of an eye
Something I must say
My heart cannot deny
Someone who cares for me
More than anything
Now that I found
What my soul was looking for
It's you and nothing more
You gave me a life
A dream comes true
It all began on the day
I fell in love with you

-My only-

I love you so much
How does one explain?
You're my forever love
Who fell into my heart?
Like the falling rain
You became my light
Within the dark
To guide my soul out
With a loving heart
You're everything to me
Special in many ways
You're my then and now
My nights and days

-Taken from me-

Why must this be?
You were taken from me
I'm left here all alone
Absorbing pain on my own
I gave you my heart
And heaven broke it apart
You always loved me
But now I must wait
Until it's time once again
To see you face to face
I will always love you
Forever more
Like two souls entwined
Mine and yours

-Precious life-

Blessed with an angel
A precious little life
Looking for loving care
And comfort when they cry
Imagine for a moment
What a mother felt
Seeing a tiny little baby
Making her heart melt
God grants miracles
From high above
Precious and beautiful
Babies to cherish and love

-My cure-

You pulled me through
My times of sadness
You were there
When there was only madness
You pulled me through
My moments of pain
You were there
When my eyes dripped like rain
In your arms I feel secure
My heart found a cure
I love you more than anyone
Feeling within I found the one

-Lonely is my night-

Lonely is my night
Before the coming day
My soul is parched
And I feel lost
In oh so many ways

Thinking of you
When you're not near
So lonely is my heart
But lonely tears
Are soon replaced
By the joy when you are here.

All this time I thought you knew
But I kept it all within
To mature and bloom
Before I could say
I honestly love you

TABLE OF CONTENTS

-Away but not gone-

Your love is with me
One part of my heart
Inside it remains
To have a special part
Your voice is now silent
My ears cannot hear
Memories left behind
Since you can't be here
In the arms of an angel
You're beyond my reach
Heaven has you now
Where I cannot see
Until we reunite again
You and me for eternity

-Come home soon-

I dream of you
While you are away
Remembering your smile
As if it were yesterday
You came into my life
Before going off to war
I dream of the day
We'll become much more
To stand before you
Exchanging our vows
So come home soon
Because our children
Miss you too

-Loving angel-

My love for you
Goes beyond the stars
Burning more than the sun
For eternity in my heart
When you're near me
Light shines upon my soul
With hope and dreams
Slowly to unfold
I go on everyday
Thanking our lord above
For sending me an angel
One so beautiful to love

-Mom and family-

Words cannot replace
How much you mean to me
A once in a life time
Loving mother I received
Although I love my family
You'll be in my heart
Always so close
Though we're far apart
It hurts to say good-bye
But I must go on
I love you mom
I'm sorry you are gone
While up in heaven
Watch over me
Until I am home
With you and the family

-A father's promise-

When you were born
Tears filled my eyes
I was overcome by joy
And yes, father's cry
We are never perfect
In any type of way
But I promise to do my best
To be here for your everyday
Now you're a woman
Independent and strong
Should you ever need me?
Don't hesitate to call

-Everything to me-

You're someone special
You came from above
Landing on my heart
Filling it with your love
You must be an angel
I see it in your eyes
With every kiss
You warm my soul inside
Heaven gave away an angel
To be here with me
You are my world
My love for eternity

-Remember us-

Please do not cry
Because I am gone
You gave my soul
A place to belong
I'll always remember
The life we shared
I can't change back time
To be with you there
From time to time
I'll look down on you
While here in heaven
My love will wait for you

-Love burns bright-

I never thought
About a new tomorrow
Then you came along
Erasing away my sorrow
Days of being alone
Became the past
I found someone special
To make love last
You've opened my heart
Shown my soul the light
I truly know now
Love can forever burn bright

-A union of two-

Below our lord above
Not as two people
Bus as a single heart in love
We exchange two rings
Along with them
One hope, one dream
To walk a path
Where our hearts and souls
Finds shelter to truly last
Guiding us along the way
Will be our memories
Of love to forever stay

-Wrongful death-

We shared so much
In this world together
And the love we had
Is gone but not forever
Because someone decided
To drink and drive
Ending our hope and dreams
For a better life
Heaven is now your home
How beautiful it must be
We will meet again
Sharing love for eternity

-Giving everything-

You're my future in life
Each morning I rise
You're in my dreams
Each night I close my eyes
You're near my soul
With each breath I take
These feeling within
Come as no mistake
I could say I love you
But that is only one part
So I'm giving you it all
From the bottom of my heart

-Never unknown-

A lot of us needed you
Many eyes have cried
If love alone was a cure
You would still be alive
As we say good-bye
Two eyes now lay closed
Only to open once more
Among heaven as your home
Everyone here misses you
But we will always know
The love you gave
Will never go unknown

-My daughter-

The day has finally come
As your father
My job is never done
I must give your hand away
To another who loves you?
Very much the same
I will miss my little girl
Gone are the days
Of you in ribbons and curls
Replaced by a young woman
Filled with hope and dreams
But daddy's little girl
Will forever live in me

Unforgiving-

Dear dad you made me sad
I lived with mom's pain
Every year it hurt so badly
When I was born
You chose to run away
Like a coward does
Leaving no words to explain
Should you ever see me?
Don't hand me your lies
The day you ran away
My coward father died

-Your beauty-

Your beauty is precious
Beyond all other things
I see it in your eyes
Making my heart sing
Whether far or near
Your love speaks softly
Through my soul's ear
Upon the shore
Or among the sea
Now and forever more
I feel you inside
The only love for me

-My beloved was taken away-

My beloved was taken away
Finding home in a higher place

Lost in sorrow it is to be
Love was pulled away from me

My beloved was taken away
Heaven made room for you today

Lost in grief words shall speak
My beautiful angel looks down on me

My beloved was taken away
I'll love you each day I'm awake

Our time together did not end
You will feel my heart someday again

Frank D. Robinson

-I once knew a man-

I once knew a man
Games were his plan
Abusing love to cripple
Hearts caring very little
Enjoying such lust
Love never to trust
Moving place to place
No care to face
Living his life
Feeling such delight
Pleasure he meets
Fate foresees
I once knew a man
Games were his plan
Lust did not last
Now buried like trash

-Honor and love-

Here are seven fresh roses
For each day of the week
Water them with care
Like you show for me
Upon the middle one
There is a diamond ring
Symbolizing the love
To make my heart complete
Now comes the time
To know another life
To honor and love you
If you will be my wife

-Some will fall-

Some will fall
This pains us all
Things they give
For freedom to live
Heroes they are
Going so far
Leaving as strangers
To fight together
Some will fall
They answered the call
For liberty and justice
Giving their all
Words will say
The sacrifice they made
For you and me
Most important their families

-A bond from birth-

He rejoiced her name
She was born today
Tears for all to see
Fell from his cheeks
Aspen dawn he gave
For all to save
His heart was filled
With love so real
Dancing with glee
From within unseen
A father people will say
But dad will forever stay

-Lover's mate-

She lies in wait with fate
To find a lover's mate
Her heart is fully grown
Blind by the unknown
Hoping she will reach
A place where souls can meet
Pushing lust aside
For love to bind
Her beauty is found
To have no bounds
Playing the part
Of a single heart
Only time will say
If fate comes her way

-From each floor-

From the top to the bottom floor
My love is here to be your door

Say my name a beat will sound
Hear my heart all around

From the top to the bottom floor
Roses lay near each door

Touch my soul with a kiss
Every day I dream of this

From the top to the bottom floor
I need you to be much more

Can you open a life with me?
You are my wife; my everything

Frank D. Robinson

-I hold in my hand-

I hold in my hand a light to see
Evermore bright should you believe?

Further to grow slow each day
Holding on with hope to stay

I hold in my hand a light to see
Alive with warmth yours to receive

What lies beyond this light?
Only you can hold it tight

I hold in my hand a part of me
It's calling out for your need

The light I reveal this day
Was my love for a long stay?

-Truly my all-

Your warmth and love
And hopes and dreams
You bring into my life
I'll always carry in me
Your beauty and smile
And eyes made with care
I'll know them well
Nothing else compares
Your soul is my pillar
And strength to stand tall
You guide my soul
To never waiver or fall

-Who you are-

You are the moon
In the nighttime
You are the sun
To my awaken days
You are the watchtower
Above my soul
Showing me the way
You are the dreams
In my mind
My life giving air
The magic in my heart
Who always is there?

TABLE OF CONTENTS

Frank D. Robinson

-Unknown place-

Lakes hold shape wind is fair
Trees of color far and near

Hills that formed small and tall
Where the sun will rise and fall

Days replaced by nights to see
The moon and stars over me

Mornings are fresh each day
Beauty beholds this land to stay

Hearing birds sing among the air
No fog or haze, only clear

Where this place is found to lie
My spirit one day will find

-Beautiful bride-

Standing down the aisle
She is beautiful and sound
Wearing white lace
Making my heart race
Roses are made and laid
In shapes of hearts today
The lights are lit
As people sit
Standing down the aisle
She is beautiful and sound
Eyes like stars
Who saved my heart?
Life begins with two
When we say, "I do"
You give your love to me
Together we will always be

Frank D. Robinson

-One day-

I kneel before the light of day
Only to speak with a voice to say

No one can steal your faith away
To deny the right for us to pray

Our spirits to meet the Lord one day
Showing us there is a home to stay

Family will come, as comfort to see
Leaving their love for us to receive

We start in life to rejoice his name
Because our faith holds no shame

We live our lives to pray each day
Our father in heaven, hear us pray

-You-

You truly are this beauty to see
There is no way I can disagree

If you see two hearts in sand
Do you place our names by hand?

You have those lips to place a kiss
To show your love will never miss

Saying no words to give my reach
I offer this love for you to see

You truly are this beauty today
How do I speak so you will stay?

Having these desires only for you
Can you stay to see them through?

-To live in heaven we will one day

To live in heaven we will one day
Family is waiting for our stay

Lives go on until called away
Angels will lead our way

To live in heaven we will one day
Our lord will know what to say

Be not afraid you came to me
Your home is waiting blessed be

To live in heaven we will one day
Free to live again our lord will say

Until that day we rejoice his name
Never to feel or walk with shame

-I need you-

Your eyes are left warm to see
Able to steal the love from me

This voice you have soft to say
To feel your lips once each day

I need this time with your grace
To touch such a beautiful face

My heart is ready for me to say
Your love I need close each day

Do you give your time for me?
I stand in wait, here to reach

My dream is clear you are seen
Each night that brings me sleep

Frank D. Robinson

She gave her life-

She wore her black today
Love was stolen away
He showed his best
But death he met

She cried at night
With burning rage
By day she makes her way
To visit where he lays

She wore her black to grieve
The love buried beneath
Kneeling before the ground
She leaves no sound

Taking pills, her body to kill
Laying atop his body still
She gave her life
Always to be his wife

-You gave me love-

You gave me love when you came
My life has never been the same

Your love will flow in my veins
To move my heart like a plane

You gave me love I feel is true
To say for sure "I love you"

I ask you now to share my life
Passing this ring to be my wife

You gave me love for words to say
Your beauty steals my breath away

You have this way to live and stay
Within my heart to carry each day

-Church is home to our lord today-

Church is home to our lord today
People will come without delay

Remember the cross as you pray
Our lord gave his life with faith

Church is home to our lord today
Your children rejoice your name

Ways to heaven start in faith
Cross your hands and look to pray

Church is home to our lord today
Heaven or earth, you guide our way

Faith gives way to find beliefs
Lord of lords we truly need

Three things-

Three things I need to say
Speaking from my heart today

First is passion to feel and see
Then with love to be complete

Second is hearts, tied in ways
Beating as one to truly stay

Third is trust for love to meet
As lives pair to feel complete

Leave our hearts find the way
To walk together in love each day

Something special comes in three
To give my all, share with me

Frank D. Robinson

-She never knew love-

I once seen this woman
Beautiful but shallow
She played with hearts
Like a game of cards

Dancing with lust
Judged looks to shove
Glamour queen, maybe
Lost for love to reach

Cruel by ways to say
Fate will be the one to play
She had the act so well
Putting hearts through hell

I once knew this woman
Beautiful but shallow
She plays no more
Dying bitter and sore

-Knowing-

Knowing with each passing night
These arms can hold you tight

Eye with eye, to stare and see
The warmth of love can truly be

Knowing with each passing day
Hearts can grow without delay

Sharing the time love can bring
Soul for soul, to dance and sing

Knowing with each day and night
Our hearts can find love in sight

The future is left unknown to see
Because love needs time to believe

-Freedom one, freedom all-

Freedom one, freedom all
Small and tall
Young or old
Something we cherish and hold
To stand with a voice
We the people of choice
Together we stand
For liberty, hand over hand
Freedom one, freedom all
We the people small and tall
To do our best
We will not rest
Stars and stripes
Our reason to fight
Day to day
Let freedom sway

-Passion-

Passion by night, for love by day
You are always in my heart, to stay

Leaving no regrets, I come to say
Knowing your touch is never far away

Passion by day, for love by night
Knowing you are close to hold in sight

Your love is special to have and see
To trust you with my hopes and dreams

Passion by night, for love by day
Your beauty takes my breath away

This search is over, my heart can see
The time and love you have for me

Frank D. Robinson
-Your passing-

You pass from this life today
To awake in heaven to stay

Eyes fill with tears of grief
Sorrow surrounds our inner being

With a heavy heart we embrace
The fact you're in a happier place

We will always have memories
Those of you and us to keep

There are no words to truly explain
Losing someone special without pain

You pass from this life today
We will see you again someday

-A story-

I have our story to read in bed
A tale to say how our love began

The day your beauty came my way
Strangers then, now lovers today

Page from page, words will speak
Step by step, lives came to meet

My story is one to say the truth
To devote my love only for you

This tale of love I read so clear
Rest your eyes, my love is near

My story ends to say good night
Placing my arms to hold you tight

-Young and brave-

He lived each day so brave
Sick inside almost everyday
Living with pain day or night
He does his best to fight
His birthday came ten today
Parents struggle inside with pain
Slow to blow the candles out
Doing his best five went out
They knew time was close
Making the best this day will go
Suddenly he felt real sick
The fever came on so quick
In the hospital on that day
He held his parents' hand to say
You did your best for me
Soon I will be cured and free

-My life-

My life has come to see this
Love and trust, nothing less

You inspire this love to stay
Finding you, it came as fate

My life will have words to say
You are everything I need today

Your touch is left for me to see
The one who shares love with me

My life is with the one to reach
I trust my heart with you to be

Angels are real for me to say
One is with my life each day

-Arms of an angel-

In the arms of an angel
You leave from here
To see another place
Spirits embrace and share
Together with friends and family
Your new home of eternal peace
An angel you became
With beautiful white wings
In the arms of an angel
Your new life begins
Leaving your love behind
Until we are together again

-Two of hearts-

She found her king
Of hearts to sing
Feeling joy inside
She was longing to find
Desire only for love
Turning away from lust
Offering her heart
For a timeless start
He found his queen
Of hearts he needs
To share a life
Caring for a beautiful wife
To have and to hold
Together as they grow old
What came from above?
Binds two souls in love

-A spirit is free-

May your spirit fly with freedom?
From all fears and cares in sight
May you find your eternal peace?
As you walk among heavens light
May the music angels play?
Be the comfort sounds you hear
As you talk to family members
May you never shed another tear?
I'll speak of our memories
And our love together in life
I will always love you
My best friend, my only wife

-Discovering love-

We knew each other
Since we were two
But as years went on
Something inside me grew
Until our high school prom
That's when I knew
What grew inside me?
Was love for you?
My life was not clear
Until that special night
When you opened my heart
With a kiss under the lights

-Two entwined-

Together we sit
Your hand upon mine
I look in your eyes
You see into mine
Our hearts are together
Like roses entwined
Forever together
One soul, one mind

-By land or sea-

By land or sea
Freedom bleeds
Our eagles fly
With liberty to fight

We send our best
Fighting unrest
Around the world
So liberty is told

By land or sea
Freedom will reach
We stand to fight
For this way of life

America will stand
Where freedom lands
From head to foot
The cause we took

Frank D. Robinson

-Immortal with time-

Immortal with time
Cursed to find
Someone with love
Unable to hide

Watching by day
Hearts to stay
Pain my soul
One so old

Immortal with time
Unable to hide
Love can free
The curse from me

She can bring to life
What denies
To beat within
My chest to rise

ABOUT THE AUTHOR

Frank lives with his wife and step-son in Pittsburgh, PA. This book was written in his spare time from work. He enjoys writing poetry and is also currently working on writing a short story.

www.ingramcontent.com/pod-product-compliance
Lightning Source LLC
Chambersburg PA
CBHW070526030426
42337CB00016B/2128